To dear Susan
and Ken,
Merry Christmas
1993
Love from Lynne
and Susan
xxxx

Australia's Outback

WELDON RUSSELL
PUBLISHING

Other titles in the series:
Australia's Animals and Wildflowers
Australia Images of a Continent

First published in Australia in 1992 by Weldon Russell Pty Ltd
107 Union Street North Sydney NSW 2060 Australia

A member of the Weldon International Group of Companies

Publisher: Elaine Russell
Managing editor: Dawn Titmus
Senior editor: Ariana Klepac
Project coordinator: Margaret Whiskin
Picture researcher: Anne Nicol
Captions: Anne Matthews
Design concept: Catherine Martin
Designer: Jean Meynert
Paste-up artist: Megan Appleby
Production: Jane Hazell, Di Leddy

National Library of Australia Cataloguing-in-Publication data

Australia's outback.

  ISBN 1 875202 48 X.

  1. Country life - Australia - Pictorial works. 2. Australia - Description
  and travel - 1976-1990 - Views. 3. Australia - Description and travel -
  1990- - Views.

994.0630222

Produced by Tien Wah Press, Singapore

A KEVIN WELDON PRODUCTION

RIGHT *The sheer walls of Kings Canyon, near Alice Springs, rise up some
270 m above the desert to form the deepest gorge in central Australia.*

FRONT COVER *Two of the huge granite rocks known as the Devil's Marbles,
which are scattered for several kilometres along the Stuart Highway to the
south of Tennant Creek. The largest of these boulders is around 7 m across.*

BACK COVER *Even in the incredible aridity of the Simpson Desert, hardy
spinifex manages to survive the harshest of conditions. The 77,000 sq km
Simpson Desert is the continent's driest region.*

ENDPAPERS *The spiky contours of a thorny devil (Moloch horridus) create
a grotesque shadow on the desert sand.*

HALF TITLE PAGE *A rustic Northern Territory 'road sign' near the Olgas
points the way to an amazingly random selection of destinations.*

OPPOSITE TITLE PAGE *Here, a solitary hardy tree rises up from an
otherwise featureless gibber plain of the Simpson Desert.*

TITLE PAGE *Many outback towns have boomed and busted, and some, like
this Western Australian settlement, now lie crumbling and completely
abandoned.*

OPPOSITE CONTENTS *Aboriginal people have long been employed as
stockmen and drovers on the cattle stations of the continent's north.*

CONTENTS *Water buffalo were introduced into the Northern Territory
in the 1820s. Today thousands of these buffalo inhabit tropical northern
Australia. They are seen here cohabiting peacefully with the black-necked
stork or jabiru.*

Australia's Outback

Contents

The Red Centre

PREVIOUS PAGES *Ayers Rock, the world's largest monolith, has many moods and tones. Although the Rock often glows like a vast red ember, its colour varies from grey to purple, depending on the light and weather conditions.*

LEFT *A full moon rises over the Olgas, while the fading light lends an air of unreality to these mysterious monoliths and their foreground of gum trees.*

BELOW *Even in the incredible aridity of the Simpson Desert, hardy trees, spinifex and mulga manage to survive the harshest of conditions. The vast Simpson Desert encompasses sections of South Australia, Queensland and the Northern Territory and is composed mainly of huge red sand ridges.*

LEFT *Brumbies, or feral horses, run wild through much of Australia. This group, photographed in the Simpson Desert, pose little threat to man, but such animals are considered to be pests in agricultural areas.*

BELOW LEFT *A dingo fence stretches into the distance behind a young girl. This structure spans the width of the continent and is designed to stop the spread of wild dogs state to state.*

BELOW RIGHT *The distinctive brilliant red flowers of the Sturt Desert Pea (Clianthus formosus), a plant which is widely distributed throughout the continent's dry interior. This is the floral emblem of South Australia.*

A group of red kangaroos (Macropus rufus) *near Alice Springs. Australia's most common kangaroo is found all over the continent and prefers an environment of scrub and grassland.*

BELOW *The ruggedly shaped quartzite walls of Ormiston Gorge, in the Northern Territory's MacDonnell Ranges, are a dramatic example of the effects of wind and water erosion.*

RIGHT *Erosion of the friable sandstone of the Olgas has created unusual rock formations, and some apparent balancing acts.*

TOP *Late afternoon light emphasises the patterns and rich terracotta tones of this Northern Territory desert sand dune.*

ABOVE *A detailed look at the famous Devil's Marbles in the Northern Territory reveals a series of smoothly rounded granite surfaces.*

RIGHT *A thorny devil pictured with the Sturt Desert Rose* (Gossypium sturtianum), *the floral emblem of the Northern Territory. Thorny devils* (Moloch horridus) *inhabit the continent's desert regions and survive exclusively on ants.*

*The spectacular
MacDonnell Ranges of
central Australia stretch
from east to west for
approximately 400 km.
These ancient quartzite
ridges and peaks form
the highlight of the striking
desert scenery around
Alice Springs.*

LEFT *Cooper Creek in outback South Australia. This irregularly flowing stream holds a special place in Australian history—as the site of camp 65 of the ill-fated 1861 Burke and Wills exploratory expedition.*

BELOW LEFT *Since the earliest days stockmen and drovers, with their well-trained horses, have been a vital component of Australia's cattle industry.*

RIGHT *Race meetings are a social highlight in the small, isolated Northern Territory settlement of Timber Creek.*

The West

PREVIOUS PAGES *Nambung National Park contains one of Australia's most peculiar geological phenomena. The Pinnacles are strangely sculpted limestone 'fingers', standing up to 6 m tall, which are scattered over a small area of this park.*

ABOVE *Rail transport, especially for freight, is still important in this vast continent. These trains are passing through Reid, a small settlement on the Nullarbor Plain.*

RIGHT *Pictured here close to the Great Australian Bight, Eyre Highway runs through the Nullarbor Plain. The Nullarbor Plain is a treeless arid plateau with extensive limestone areas with a total area of 260,000 sq km. It stretches from south-west South Australia to south-east Western Australia.*

LEFT *Western Australia's Cape Le Grand National Park, to the east of Esperance, contains a wide variety of scenery. Coastal bays, granite peaks and forest-lined inlets are all components of this lovely but little-known wilderness area.*

BELOW *The blue-tongued lizard* (Tiliqua scinoides) *lives on berries, insects and snails—it grows to approximately 30 cm long.*

These old pearl-sorting sheds in Broome, Western Australia, demonstrate a very basic architectural style. Broome is one of the world's pearling capitals.

A group of station hands at a rodeo in Broome. These exciting events are important sporting and social occasions in many rural regions of Australia.

The unmistakable beehive-shaped forms of the Bungle Bungle Range in Western Australia's Kimberleys. Centuries of weathering have rounded the range's surfaces and eaten away at the fragile sandstone.

BELOW *Unlike the saltwater crocodile, the smaller freshwater crocodile* (Crocodyius johnstoni) *is not aggressive towards humans, although it preys on a wide range of fish and other animal life. It is found in creeks, freshwater rivers and billabongs across the north of Australia.*

RIGHT *Windjana Gorge in the Napier Range of the West Kimberley region. In the wet season a river flows through this 4 km long limestone gorge. It has long been regarded as a sacred site by Aboriginal people.*

ABOVE *Despite the north-west's extreme climate and arid soils, springtime almost miraculously produces desert blooms like these. Such plants have adapted to survive even the most rugged conditions.*

LEFT *Geikie Gorge is one of the Kimberleys' most spectacular and famous attractions. The Fitzroy River flows through this 10 km long valley, the ancient limestone walls of which change colour from red to gold according to the time of day.*

ABOVE *Four-wheel drive vehicles are the only way to see some of the more remote areas of Australia where the condition of unsealed roads is unpredictable.*

RIGHT *Hannan Street, Kalgoorlie, Western Australia, contains some interesting examples of country town architecture. The main thoroughfare of this prosperous gold mining centre is named after Patrick Hannan who discovered gold in the region in 1893.*

The magnificent King George River has carved its way through the lime-stone plateau of the East Kimberley region and flows into the Timor Sea north-west of Wyndham.

LEFT *Chichester Range National Park, in Western Australia's Pilbara region, consists of vast plains dotted with ancient volcanic rock outcrops.*

RIGHT *Life in the outback can be harsh, but children like this Western Australian Aboriginal girl enjoy space and freedom that city dwellers would find difficult to comprehend.*

BELOW RIGHT *First explored in the 1870s, the Great Sandy Desert, in the north of Western Australia, was later part of the Canning Stock Route. For many years this arid region was crossed by countless drovers and their cattle.*

Kakadu and Arnhem Land

ABOVE *A beautiful specimen of the lotus lily* (Nelumbo nucifera), *with its large flat leaves, photographed in Kakadu National Park. This plant prefers tropical, deep-water environments, and flowers during the dry season.*

RIGHT *A young Aboriginal girl harvests waterlilies* (Nymphaea) *at a billabong in central Arnhem Land. The seeds, stems and corms of these lilies are edible.*

PREVIOUS PAGES *Misty morning light bathes this tranquil river scene in the sacred Kakadu National Park. Kakadu, in the 'Top End' of the Northern Territory, was a gift to Australia of 6144 sq km from its traditional Aboriginal owners.*

At the height of the monsoon season, Kakadu's tree-covered lowlands are transformed into what appears to be a vast lake.

LEFT *This rugged rocky scenery is part of the 97,000 sq km expanse of the Northern Territory's Arnhem Land. This Aboriginal reserve has been inhabited by indigenous Australians for at least 25,000 years.*

ABOVE RIGHT *Dance and ritual have always been important in Aboriginal society, and body decoration with ochre, clays and kaolin is an integral aspect of such ceremonies.*

BELOW RIGHT *Throughout northern and central Australia many caves and rock shelters, once used as semi-permanent dwellings by Aboriginal people, are decorated with fascinating ochre-coloured examples of primitive artwork.*

ABOVE *The perentie (Varanus giganteus), Australia's largest goanna, reaches lengths of up to 2.5 m. Found in the most arid regions, this well-camouflaged lizard lives on small marsupials, birds, other lizards, snakes and insects.*

RIGHT *During the 'wet', waterfalls tumble off the 300 m high Kakadu escarpment, which borders the low, flood-prone plains of Kakadu National Park.*

LEFT *The South Alligator River flows northward through Kakadu National Park on its way into Van Diemen Gulf. This river, along with its companion, the West Alligator, was named in 1820 in the mistaken belief that alligators, rather than crocodiles, inhabited its waters.*

ABOVE *The pied or magpie goose (Anseranas semipalmata) is found only in the north of Australia and often travels in flocks of up to 100,000. This bird has distinctive black and white plumage, set off by orange-coloured legs.*

After the 'rains', water-
falls like this one abound
in the spectacular Kakadu
National Park.

LEFT *Tranquil billabongs such as this are a common feature of the wetlands of northern Australia.*

RIGHT *Dramatic variations in the climate of northern Australia transform wet season floodplains into dried-out flats during the dry months.*

BELOW *A saltwater or estuarine crocodile (Crocodylus porosus) slides, open-jawed, into a Northern Territory river. Although these large reptiles prefer saltwater, they can travel long distances up rivers and pose a threat to the unwary traveller.*

Gulf Country
to the Riverina

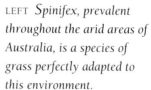

LEFT *Spinifex, prevalent throughout the arid areas of Australia, is a species of grass perfectly adapted to this environment.*

BELOW LEFT *An emu (Dromaius novaeholiandiae) wanders among the saltbushes and other stunted vegetation at the Willandra Lakes region of south-western New South Wales. This semi-arid area was once covered with water and abounded in aquatic and plant life.*

RIGHT *The ancient limestone outcrops of Royal Arch Caves National Park, near Chillagoe in northern Queensland, contain a labyrinthine network of passages and caverns. The largest cave, Royal Arch, is over 50 m long and some 12 m high.*

PREVIOUS PAGES *The plains bordering the Gulf of Carpentaria—at the very tip of Australia—are covered by a maze of rivers and channel systems. In the wet season it becomes a floodplain.*

LEFT *Sheep shearing in the traditional manual style is skilled and strenuous work, and a gradually dying art. Many farmers now use machinery as a modern alternative.*

RIGHT *Outback sheep farming poses many problems—the most serious of which is drought. This Riverina property is fortunate enough to still have water in its dam, despite the parched conditions.*

BELOW RIGHT *The Australian outback has spawned some unique characters, such as this Queensland dingo trapper. Dingoes are considered a threat to livestock in many parts of Australia and trapping is therefore a widespread activity.*

Wind erosion has created a strangely patterned desert landscape in the Willandra Lakes region of outback New South Wales.

ABOVE LEFT *The frilled lizard (Chlamydosaurus kingii) is found across northern Australia. When it is alarmed its large frill of skin, which normally lies loosely around its neck, is raised in a defiant display of aggression.*

ABOVE RIGHT *The spirited colours of these blossoms are an example of the diversity of flora and fauna found in tropical Queensland.*

LEFT *Sunset over a woolshed in outback New South Wales.*

LEFT *An aerial view of Birdsville, near the border of Queensland and South Australia. This once bustling customs post and overnight stopping place for stockmen is now a sleepy town with just a handful of residents and a lone hotel.*

ABOVE RIGHT *Residents of Birdsville create some excitement by staging an outback-style cricket match.*

BELOW RIGHT *The focus of social life in isolated Birdsville is the town's much-photographed single-storey pub.*

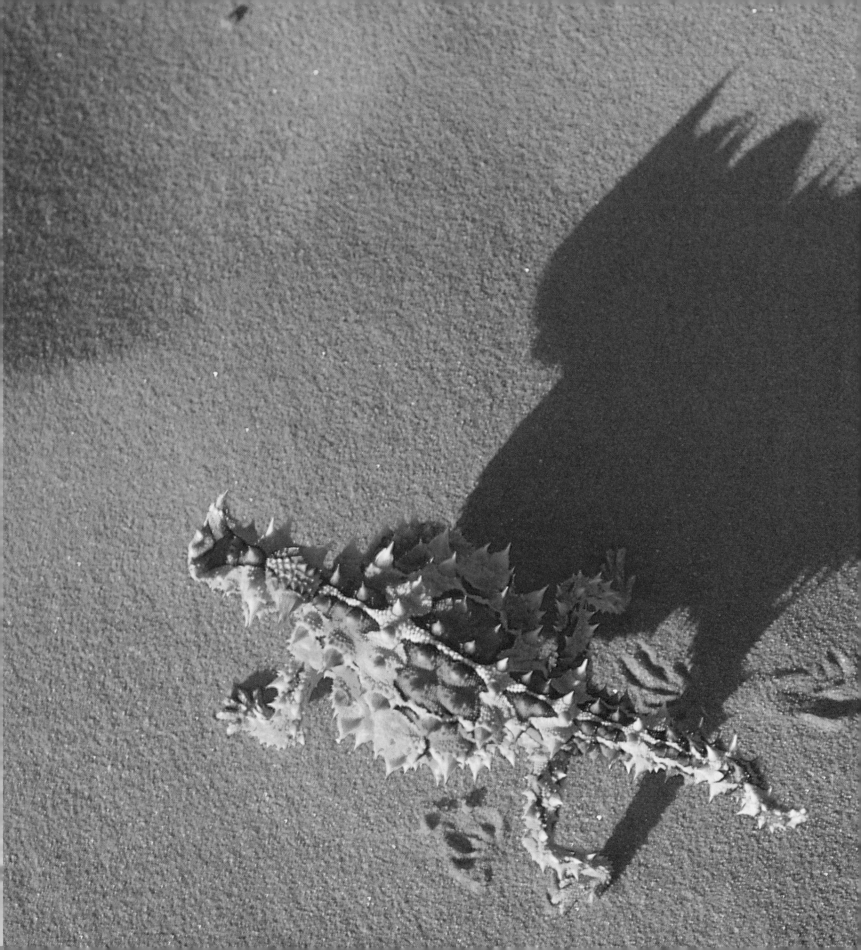